KATHARINE PAULAHA BROWN

COOKBOOK

*First we add some heavy cream &
then we lighten it up with some butta'*

Prized Family Recipes

ISBN 978-0-9907082-4-7

Second Printing

First published 2020 by Patron Books

PATRON BOOKS

I want to dedicate this book to those
who bring love and joy to my life:

My role model, best friend and father, Dr. Dennis Frank Paulaha, and my loving and caring mother, Deborah Susan Paulaha

My best friend and sister, Sarah Paulaha Schwartz, and my brother in law, Stephen Schwartz

My soul mate and husband, Craig

My Godparents, Drs. James and Vicki Mayer

My Aunt, Pam Brown

My sisters, Cadence Paulaha and Emily Reineke

My Cat Molly

My sister's first love, Bear (a Havanese)

And to those I have lost, but will never forget:

My Paulaha and Gamelin grandparents

Richard Paulaha, my uncle

Auntie Ann

Russel and Alice Hatling

Bob and Mary Robinson

Lorraine and Bob Martin

"Everything you see I owe to spaghetti."
- Sophia Loren

"I only drink Champagne on two occasions, when I am in love and when I am not."
- Coco Chanel

"Life is too short for fake butter or fake people."
- Julia Child

"Take care of all your memories. For you cannot relive them."
- Bob Dylan

"Family is the most important thing in the world."
- Princess Diana

"You can discover more about a person in an hour of play, than a year of conversation."
- Plato

"As you get older, you realize there are no answers. Just stories."
- Anonymous

"Cooking is like painting or writing a song. Just as there are so many notes or colors, there are only so many flavors - it's how you combine them that sets you apart."
- Wolfgang Puck

"The only time to eat diet food is waiting for the steak to cook."
- Julia Child

"A lot of good arguments are spoiled by some fool who knows what he is talking about."
- Miguel de Unamuno

"Principles are like prayers. Noble of course, but awkward at a party."
- Downton Abbey

Contents

Contents

Introduction

As long as I can remember, I loved to be in the kitchen. When I was a little girl, my family lived in a John Howe/Frank Lloyd Wright home on Lake Minnetonka in Deephaven, Minnesota. From the carport, there was a swinging door allowing you to push groceries right through to the kitchen instead of hauling them through the house. However, I truly believed it was the quickest way to get me into the kitchen as well. I remember as a little girl sitting on the counter helping with anything I could, from mixing up a batch of Spritz cookies with my mom for the holidays, doing the dishes, rolling out dough for Kolache, buffing flatware, making Mickey Mouse pancakes, peeling carrots, or flipping burgers on the stove top. I also vividly remember the day when I accidentally turned my head too quickly and got my hair tangled in the KitchenAid standing mixer.

My family moved a lot growing up. We spent time in Minnesota and Vermont, but we spent the most time in Hudson, Wisconsin. In Hudson, I found an interest in baking cakes and decorating each and every one with flowers and pretty designs. To this day, I do not remember my dad ever turning down a piece. One year, my younger sister, Sarah and I both asked for Easy-Bake Ovens for Christmas. We must have been good girls that year, because Santa granted our wish on Christmas morning. The Easy-Bake Ovens mentioned a 100 watt light bulb, but we assumed that the bulb was so you could see how your dish looked as it was cooking, like normal ovens. After waiting for nearly an hour for my brownie to cook, I realized that the 100 watt bulb was indeed a requirement.

When I was 14 years old, I decided to get in to the restaurant business and started my first job working in a restaurant in Hudson, Wisconsin. It was called Chadwick's. It is no longer there, but I learned a lot bussing tables and hosting in a fine dining restaurant. For one, I knew I loved hosting, serving, and seeing people come celebrate birthdays, anniversaries, a new job or promotion, a special family event, or just a night out on the town. I think this experience is what kept me working in the bar and restaurant industry for nearly 15 years, even while I was attending the University of St. Thomas in St. Paul, Minnesota. Working in the bar and restaurant industry is also where I met my husband and some of my very best friends to this very day.

Growing up, holidays were important to me and I knew what to expect for each holiday, year after year. I remember every Christmas Eve we went over to my dad's side of the family, to Lorraine and Bob's. It was always the same people every year, probably 60 of us. Card tables in many colors and mismatched chairs and folding tables were in every room of the house. An assortment of fabric and plastic holiday table cloths were used on many of the tables. I remember the dining room turned into the center stage buffet table where there were always at least two turkeys and two hams. Everyone would bring a dish to share or a dessert. My mom would always make Kolache and Spritz cookies. I remember they had two living rooms and a big glass porch. The porch is where the Christmas tree went and where we opened gifts together after dinner. They had a pool table in a billiard room in the basement. I remember one year my Uncle Rick gave my cousins, Blake and Peder, these slimy gooey slugs. And, as you can imagine, my sister and I spent that night being chased by slimy slugs. I guess boys will be boys. As time went on, we lost many loved ones including Lorraine and Bob, and the traditions slowly ended. I will always remember Christmas Eve with family in Lorraine and Bob's home and the memories will always remain near and dear to me. On Christmas, we typically went to my Aunt Bev and Wayne's home. I remember each year, after a delicious feast, we all worked together to get a group picture. My Uncle Rick would coordinate all thirty or so cameras on a hutch or side table. Each person would gather around their own camera and in unison would hit the timer button and run back as quickly as they could to make the photo. I still have some of those photos. Most are action shots of people still running or falling over.

Today, I live in an an old Tudor in South Minneapolis in the Fulton Neighborhood, with my amazing husband, Craig and our black and white cat, Molly. Since we have been in our home, we have hosted countless murder mystery dinner parties, lobster parties, holiday feasts, Christmas Eve open houses, Italian nights, meat and potatoes nights, family picnics, an after wedding brunch for my sister, Friendsgiving, Friester, pizza parties, and fondu parties. I love pulling out all of the Warren MacKenzie pottery dishes that my parents collected for me over the years. We visited his art studio often growing up, and he even had a kids' section of small pots that we use for olives and nuts today. I inherited a large collection of Noritake China, which is also fun to pull out for any kind of get together.

I find myself coming up with new party ideas just to get my friends and family in the same room. I love seeing people come together, sharing a bottle of wine, clinking glasses, cheering over a bottle of Prosecco, celebrating promotions and new chapters, laughing or sharing stories and memories together around a dinner table or in the backyard. There is something so special about dining in. Perhaps it is people cooking together and working together to create a meal for all to share. Or, perhaps it is because it is a casual place to relax and kick back. All over the world, people come together around food and drink to celebrate life, which is what ultimately inspired me to write this book. Over the last ten years or so, I have started and stopped trying to write a cookbook. I never quite knew exactly what style or template to use. I finally realized it should not really matter if I have the best staged photos or if I have paid a staff a lot of money to make up recipes or write my copy. My decision was to write a cookbook of my favorite and go to recipes to share with others.

As time goes on, you lose loved ones and traditions and holidays tend to fall apart. I believe this is one of the hardest things I have had to cope with as I have gotten older. I wanted to have a cookbook to share with my friends and family in hopes these recipes would get passed down after me. This cookbook consists of recipes that have led to some of my most cherished memories, which remain near and dear to my heart. I hope you can find joy making these dishes as I have over the years.

I suppose if you are wondering where the title comes from, I'll tell you. It came from a dinner date with friends at a restaurant in New Orleans years ago. Our waiter, Raymond, used this phrase as to how they made their famous BBQ shrimp sauce. It was a memorable night filled with great food and amazing wine. To this day, when we get together or cook a meal together, we reminisce about this night.

Disclaimer: Some of the following recipes have been passed down to me from my mother, family members and friends. Most were on old yellowed crisp and faded index and recipe cards that have seen a lot of love. I do not know where they originated or how old they may be.

My Father

I suppose I wrote this book for my father, Dr. Dennis Frank Paulaha, who is and forever will be my best friend and role model. He is an artist at heart, and I think that is how I found my love for houses and the art world. Ever since I can remember, he told me stories and was always writing. When we lived in Deephaven, Minnesota, he spent a lot of time at Hart's Cafe/Sunsets in Wayzata writing newsletters and books. I always wanted to follow in his footsteps.

My father has B.S. and M.A. degrees in economics from the University of Minnesota and a Ph.D. in economics from the University of Washington with a specialization in environmental economics. As a college and university professor, he taught macroeconomic and microeconomic theory at the principles, intermediate, advanced and graduate level, monetary theory and policy, environmental economics, and special issues courses.

Some books by Dr. D.F. Paulaha

An American Child's Portfolio: The Art of Saving and Investing for
Children
Calendar of Days
The Triangle and the Beautiful Circle
The Tumbler
Making Squares
Rubber Ducky Economics
The Market: A Really Bad Idea
Politics & Economics
How to Solve Economic Problems
Economics Without Markets
Elephant Droppings
How to Spin Gold into Straw
American Freedom

Baking Requires Measuring. Cooking Requires Experimentation.

Liquids

Cup (C)   Tablespoon (T)   teaspoon (t)

1 C	16 T	48 t
3/4 C	12 T	36 t
2/3 C	10 T, 2 t	32 t
1/2 C	8 T	24 t
1/3 C	5 T, 1 t	16 t
1/4 C	4 T	12 t
1/8 C	2 T	6 t
1/16 C	1 T	3 t

Dry

Cup (C)   Fluid Ounce (fl oz / oz)   Tablespoon (T) / teaspoon (t)   Milliliter (ml)

1 C	18 oz	16 T	237 ml
3/4 C	6 oz	12 T	177 ml
2/3 C	5.3 oz	10 T, 2 t	158 ml
1/2 C	4 oz	8 T	118 ml
1/3 C	2.7 oz	5 T, 1 t	79 ml
1/4 C	2 oz	4 T	59 ml
1/8 C	1 oz	2 T	30 ml
1/16 C	1/2 oz	1 T	15 ml

Appetizers
& Beverages
& Sides

Broccoli Summer Salad

2 lb fresh broccoli florets, cut into bite-size pieces

1/2 c cherry tomatoes

1 lb bacon, cooked and crumbled

1/2 c dried cranberries

1/4 c red onion, chopped finely

1/2 c sunflower seed nuts

2 T sugar

2 T white vinegar

1 c mayonnaise

1/4 c blue cheese or feta crumbles (optional)

In a small mixing bowl, combine the sugar, vinegar, and mayonnaise. Mix well. Set aside.

In a large mixing bowl, combine the broccoli, cherry tomatoes, bacon, cranberries, red onion, and sunflower seeds. Toss with dressing and chill overnight.

Truffle Popcorn

This is one of my favorite snacks. It is rich and delicious, and great for movie nights in the backyard.

White popped popcorn

Pecorino Romano cheese, grated

Black or white truffle oil

Salt and pepper

Drizzle truffle oil over popcorn. Toss to lightly cover the popcorn. Add cheese. Salt and pepper to taste.

Potato Salad

3 lb peeled and cooked just to tender potatoes still warm. Cut into bite-size cubes (red potatoes or any kind you prefer).

3 hard boiled eggs, lightly chopped

1 c celery, diced

1/4 c red onion, chopped

2 T pimentos, diced

1 T white vinegar

2 T yellow mustard

2 c mayonnaise

1 1/2 t fresh ground black pepper

1 T salt

1/2 c sugar

Place the potatoes in a large mixing bowl. Drape with towel to keep warm.

Mix the vinegar, mustard, and mayonnaise in a small bowl. Set aside.

In another mixing bowl, combine the pepper, salt and sugar. Pour over potatoes and toss lightly to coat. Add mayonnaise mixture and toss lightly to coat. Add the eggs, celery, and pimentos. Toss lightly to mix. Refrigerate overnight and serve chilled.

Sabelhaus Nantucket Crab Dip

While visiting great family friends in Nantucket, MA, the Sabelhaus family, they hosted a grand house warming party. They made this wonderful appetizer dip that is just out of this world. Each time I make it, I think of all the memories I have on Nantucket with the Sabelhaus family.

1 package softened regular cream cheese

1 c real mayonnaise

2 T minced dried onions

Couple dashes of garlic powder

Swigs of Tabasco and Worcestershire sauce

1 12 jar Heinz Chili Sauce

1 8 oz can whole crab lump meat, drained

1 box Triscuit crackers

In a bowl, mix cream cheese, onions, garlic powder, Tabasco, and Worcestershire sauce. Spread on platter. Refrigerate until chilled.

Spread Heinz Chili Sauce on top.

Top with drained crab.

Serve chilled with Triscuit crackers.

Char Broiled Oysters

2 1/2 sticks butter, very soft

1 t salt

1/2 t white pepper

2 1/2 t fresh ground black pepper

2 T fresh garlic, minced

1/2 t cayenne pepper

1/2 lemon, juiced

1 T fresh parsley, chopped

1 c Pecorino Romano cheese, grated

2 dozen oysters, shucked with juices in shell

In a bowl, mix together the butter, salt, white pepper, pepper, garlic, cayenne, lemon juice, parsley, and 1/2 the cheese.

Shuck and place the oysters on an oyster rack. Try to keep the juices in the shell with the oyster while shucking. Put oysters on heated grill. Cook for 3 minutes. Add a dollop of the butter batter to each oyster. Cook another 3-5 minutes or until the edges become lightly brown and bubbly. Sprinkle with remaining cheese on top and remove from grill. Garnish with parsley. Serve with lemon wedges and crusty bread for dipping.

Velvet Hammer

This is a perfect drink for a chilly night in the hot tub. It tastes like chocolate milk.

1 oz vodka

1/2 oz KAHLUA

1/2 oz Baileys Irish cream

2 oz skim milk (or cream)

2 oz soda water

Combine all ingredients in a glass. Fill with ice. Stir gently. Serve.

Orange Julius

I used to make this for my dad and me. It is such a treat.

1 12 oz can frozen orange juice from concentrate

1 c milk

1 1/2 c ice cubes

1/2 c water

1 t vanilla

2 T powdered sugar

Orange for garnish

Combine all ingredients in a blender. Blend until all ingredients are frothy. Serve with an orange slice.

Brussels Sprouts

I have to give my sister credit for this recipe. My husband thought he hated Brussels sprouts and refused to touch them with a 10 foot pole. My sister made these one night for dinner and basically shoved them in my husband's mouth. To this day, we still laugh about it He now requests this side at least once a week.

4 c Brussels sprouts

3 stripes bacon, cooked and crumbled

Extra virgin olive oil or avocado oil

Fresh parmesan cheese, finely shredded

Cayenne pepper

Garlic salt

Fresh ground black pepper

Cut the ends off the Brussels sprouts, then cut them in half.

Lightly toss the Brussels sprouts in olive oil. Season with garlic salt and pepper. Spread in a single layer on a baking sheet. Top with cheese, crumbled cooked bacon, and some dashes of cayenne.

Preheat oven to 350 degrees. Bake, tossing once, until they are a bit toasty and cooked through. Can be served hot or cold.

(My sister cooks the Brussels sprouts for 15 to 20 minutes before adding the cheese, bacon, and cayenne.)

Green Bean Casserole

A must have for Thanksgiving and Christmas.

2 10.5 oz cans cream of mushroom soup

1 c skim milk

2 t soy sauce

1/2 t fresh ground black pepper

6 c fresh blanched green beans (or 4 14.5 oz cans green beans)

1/2 c mushrooms, chopped

1 1/2 c fried onions

Mix soup, milk, soy sauce, black pepper, and 1/2 the fried onions in a casserole dish. Stir in the green beans and mushrooms.

Preheat over to 350 degrees. Bake for 25 minutes. Sprinkle the rest of the fried onions on top of the casserole and cook for another 10 minutes or until onions are golden brown.

Punch

This is one of the most delicious punch recipes I have ever had. We made this for our pirate murder mastery dinner party and added dry ice. I also made it for my girlfriend's baby shower. Great for Halloween or birthday parties.

1 3 oz package of raspberry Jell-O gelatin mix

1 3 oz package of strawberry Jell-O gelatin mix

1 3 oz package of cranberry Jell-O gelatin mix

2 c sugar

8 c boiling water

2 46 oz cans pineapple juice

2 c lemon juice

2 2 liters ginger ale

1 orange, sliced

1 lemon, sliced

1 lime, sliced

Dry ice (optional)

Combine gelatin and sugar. Add to the boiling water and stir until dissolved. Stir in pineapple and lemon juice. Freeze until frosty, not frozen solid. In a punch bowl, take half the juice mixture and pour 2 liters of ginger ale on top. Garnish with fruit slices.

Christmas Gelatin Shots

This recipe was an experiment using what we had on hand, but they are really quite delicious.

1 3 oz package raspberry gelatin dissolved in 1 c boiling water. Add 1 c blueberry vodka. Mix well.

1 3 oz package lime gelatin dissolved in 1 c boiling water. Add 1 c citron vodka. Mix well.

Fill shot glasses with one of the above. You can also do half and half, so you have half with green on the bottom and half with red on the bottom. Chill the first layer for a couple hours until set. Add the other layer on top to fill the shot glass. Make sure the second layer is cool enough to not melt the first layer. Chill until firm.

Pumpkin Seeds

This is a great pumpkin seed recipe for the fall. My husband absolutely loves this recipe.

4 c fresh pumpkin seeds

6 c water

4 T salt

Cayenne pepper

Garlic salt

Fresh ground black pepper

Lawry's Seasoned Salt

Rinse the freshly pulled pumpkin seeds under cold water in a colander to clean them as best you can.

In a pot, add water and seeds. Bring water and seeds to a boil. Add salt. Boil for 10 minutes. Remove from heat and drain seeds.

Toss seeds in olive oil. Spread the seeds on a cookie sheet. Sprinkle with a few dashes of cayenne, garlic salt, fresh ground black pepper, and seasoned salt.

Bake at 400 degrees. Make sure to toss the seeds every 5-10 minutes until seeds are a light golden brown. Once cooled, store in air-tight container.

Sarah's Artichoke Dip

My sister is a fabulous cook. Always has been. I have always looked up to her as to how she can throw something together on a whim, without looking at a recipe or measuring anything. I always bring this dish when we go to the Macdonald family cabin on the St. Croix River in the summer.

1 8 oz package regular cream cheese, softened

1/4 c real mayonnaise

1/4 c parmesan cheese, grated

1/4 c Pecorino Romano cheese, grated

2 cloves garlic, minced

3/4 t dried basil

1/2 t garlic salt

Salt and pepper to taste

1 14 oz can artichokes, drained and slightly chopped

1/2 c frozen chopped spinach, thawed and drained

1/2 c mozzarella cheese, shredded

Tortilla chips or a crusty baguette for serving

Mix the first 8 ingredients together. Mix in the artichokes and spinach. Top with mozzarella. Bake at 350 degrees for 25 minutes or until cheese is golden brown and bubbly. Serve with chips or crusty bread.

Cream Cheese Stuffed Jalapeños

12 Jalapeño peppers cut in half lengthwise, seeded

5 slices bacon, cooked and crumbled

1 8 oz package cream cheese (regular or light)

1/2 c cheddar cheese, shredded

1/4 c green onions, minced

2 t fresh lime juice

1/2 can diced tomatoes, drained

In a bowl, mix together cream cheese, lime juice, and green onions. Fill the jalapeños with mixture. Top with bacon, diced tomatoes, and cheddar cheese.

Bake at 350 degrees or grill on indirect medium heat until jalapeños are lightly charred and heated through.

Taco Dip

A woman I worked with for years would always make this dish for potlucks and social events in the office. It's delicious.

16 oz cream cheese, at room temperature

16 oz sour cream

1 1.25 oz packet original taco seasoning

2 c iceberg lettuce, shredded

1 c fresh tomatoes, diced (or canned)

2 c cheddar cheese, finely shredded

3/4 c black olives, sliced

Tortilla chips

In a bowl, using a hand mixer, whip the cream cheese thoroughly. Add sour cream and taco seasoning and mix until well blended. Spread evenly on a plate. Chill at least 2 hours. Before serving, top with lettuce, tomatoes, cheese, and olives. Serve with tortilla chips.

You can always add a base layer of refried beans, or top with black beans, Jalapeños, sliced Pepperoncini peppers, grilled chicken, or corn.

Paulaha Spiced Cider

My mother made this every Christmas and Thanksgiving. I cannot remember a holiday without it. I loved the way it made the house smell. Each time I make this, it brings back so many memories watching and cheering "the dumb guys" (Minnesota Vikings) on football Sundays with my dad.

1/2 or a full gallon of cider

1 orange

Whole cloves

Cinnamon sticks

Place the cider in a pot and place it on the stove top on low. Pierce the orange with about 50-75 whole cloves and set in the cider with a few cinnamon sticks. You can leave this on all day and keep replenishing the cider as it goes.

Southside Cocktail

1 12 oz can frozen limeade from concentrate

1 12 oz can frozen lemonade from concentrate

Gin or vodka

Soda water

Handful of fresh mint

Lime wedges

Combine the limeade, lemonade, and handful of fresh mint in a blender or food processor. Mix until well blended.

Mix 1/4 c of mix with 2 oz of gin or vodka. Top with 4 oz - 8 oz of soda water. Garnish with mint and a lime wedge.

Sautéed Vegetables

1 green zucchini, sliced

1 yellow zucchini, sliced

1/2 red onion, roughly chopped

1/2 white onion, roughly chopped

1 c Baby Bella Mushrooms, rinsed and sliced

1 c cherry tomatoes

Salt and fresh ground black pepper to taste

1/2 t garlic powder

3 T extra virgin olive oil

In a skillet over medium heat add the extra virgin olive oil and heat for 2 minutes. Add the onions and sauté for 3 minutes, stirring frequently. Add remaining vegetables and garlic powder. Salt and pepper to taste. Stir and cook for another 5 minutes or until vegetables are tender. Serve immediately.

Crab Cakes

My husband and I make these crab cakes for date night or when we host lobster night or seafood night. They go great with char broiled oysters and crusty bread. It is one of my all time favorite dishes to make.

4 cans lump white crab meat, drained

1/2 c Ritz Crackers, crushed

4 green onions, finely chopped

3/4 c green bell pepper, finely chopped

1/3 c real mayonnaise

1 egg

1 t Worcestershire sauce

1 t dry mustard

1/2 t fresh lemon juice

1/4 t garlic, minced

1 t Old Bay Seasoning

1/2 c quality butter, melted

Panko Bread Crumbs

Spicy aioli or tartar sauce for dipping

Lemons for garnish

Fresh parsley for garnish

Directions for Crab Cakes

Mix the crab, crushed crackers, green onions, green bell pepper, mayonnaise, egg, Worcestershire sauce, dry mustard, lemon juice, garlic, and Old Bay seasoning together in a mixing bowl. Chill overnight or for at least 1 hour.

Preheat oven to 400 degrees.

Melt butter and mark on baking sheet with a pastry brush where the crab cakes will go. The recipe will make 4-6 crab cakes depending on how large you make them. Roll the crab cake into a ball and roll it in the bread crumbs. Press on pan and drizzle with some melted butter.

Bake about 15 minutes, until the bottom is golden brown. Flip once and cook until bottom is golden brown. Garnish with parsley. Serve with lemon wedges and spicy lemon aioli.

Roasted Red Potatoes

1 lb baby red potatoes, quartered

1/2 white onion, chopped

3 T extra virgin olive oil or avocado oil

1 T fresh rosemary

1 T fresh thyme

1/2 t garlic salt

1/2 t Lawry's Seasoned Salt

Place the potatoes in a stock pot. Add water until the potatoes are completely submerged. Bring to a boil and cook until you can start to poke a fork through the potatoes. Drain the potatoes.

In a skillet, heat olive oil over medium heat. Add potatoes. Add onions. Add seasonings. Stir occasionally until potatoes are golden brown on all sides.

Grilled Asparagus

This is great side to pair with lamb or turkey

1 lb fresh asparagus

1/4 c extra virgin olive oil

3 T garlic, minced

1/4 t garlic salt

1/4 fresh ground black pepper

1/2 lemon, squeezed

In a bowl, soak the asparagus in cold water for 15-20 minutes.

In a small bowl, combine the olive oil, garlic, salt, pepper, and lemon juice. Stir with a rubber basting brush. Once grill is hot, place asparagus on grill and baste with the oil mixture. Flip. Repeat. Cook until asparagus has grill marks or until cooked to your liking. Serve immediately.

Craig's Legendary Sticky Wings

These legendary sticky wings fall off the bone and continue to be a crowd favorite, especially on game days or guy's nights.

12 full chicken wings, rinsed well and patted dry

6 oz pineapple juice

12 oz teriyaki sauce

4 oz soy sauce (or low sodium)

2 dashes of liquid smoke

3 T brown sugar

In a large mixing bowl, mix all the ingredients together. Add the wings. Put in fridge to marinate for at least 45 minutes, but no longer than 2 hours.

Place wings bone side down on a rimmed baking sheet. Pour 1/3 of the leftover marinade over the wings. Set the remaining marinade in the fridge for later. Dome wings with aluminum foil. Bake at 275 degrees for 2 hours. Remove from oven.

Take the wings and the drippings from the baking sheet and combine with the leftover marinade. Preheat grill to medium heat. Once grill is preheated, place the wings bone side down on the grill. Flip wings four times, each time dunking the wings back into the marinade. Wings are done when they become sticky. Serve immediately.

Sautéed Spinach

Wonderful side with steak or seafood.

1 lb spinach

1 t extra virgin olive oil

1/2 t red pepper flakes

1/4 t garlic salt

2 cloves garlic, sliced thin

Heat a Dutch oven or large skillet over medium heat. Add olive oil and garlic. Cook and stir for one minute. Add spinach, red pepper flakes, and garlic salt.

Cook for 3-5 minutes, stirring frequently until spinach is dark green and cooked through.

Queso Dip

I received this yummy queso taco dip recipe from one of my oldest friends, Becky. As roommates, we spent many nights making taco salads, paninis and eating taco dip together.

1 12.5 oz can premium white chicken breast, drained

1 10 oz can Rojo diced tomatoes, with green chillies

1 16 oz jar salsa (mild, medium or hot)

1 16 oz Kraft Velveeta Original Cheese

1 1.25 oz packet original taco seasoning

1 15 oz can chili with beans (or without beans)

Cayenne pepper or Tabasco (optional)

Tortilla chips

Add all ingredients to a slow cooker on low. Heat and stir until all ingredients are mixed well and hot. Serve with tortilla chips.

Fruit Dip

1 8 oz package cream cheese

1 7 oz jar of marshmallow cream

1 .23 oz Kool-Aid Lemonade packet

1 8 oz container Cool Whip

Seasonal fruit, such as:

Blackberries

Bananas (tossed in lemon juice to prevent browning)

Strawberries

Pineapple

Toothpicks

In a mixing bowl, mix the top three ingredients together. Fold in the Cool Whip. Serve with fresh fruit and toothpicks.

Breakfast

My Mom's French Toast

6-8 slices of Vienna bread, day old (frozen works great)

3 eggs, beaten slightly

Tabasco

Salt and pepper

Safflower oil

Powdered sugar

Maple syrup

Fresh strawberries

On a plate, lightly whisk the eggs with a couple dashes of Tabasco. Salt and pepper to taste.

In a frying pan, add enough safflower oil to cover the pan roughly 1/2". Heat oil over medium heat. Once the oil is heated, take a couple pieces of bread at a time and cover them thoroughly in egg batter. Place in oil and fry until golden brown. Then flip. Once both sides are golden brown, remove from pan and place on plate. Sprinkle with powdered sugar, drizzle with maple syrup, and top with fresh strawberries.

Dad's Bagel

I remember my dad making this bagel combo for any meal of the day. I know they sell strawberry cream cheese in the store, but trust me, it is not even close to the same thing.

Plain or sesame bagel

Strawberry jam

Plain cream cheese

Toast the bagel to your liking. Spread with cream cheese. Top with strawberry jam. Serve warm.

Fresh Morning Juice

This is a delicious juice recipe. We make this in our Omega juicer and it is so delicious.

10-12 carrots, cut into 3" pieces

1/2 pineapple with skin and core removed and cut into slender pieces

1 lemon, peeled

2 large oranges, peeled and sliced into wedges

4 oz fresh ginger

Juice carrots first, followed by juicing the fruit and ginger. Stir and enjoy.

Crepes

A good non-stick 12" or 15" skillet

3/4 c all-purpose flour

1/2 t salt

1 t baking powder

2 T powdered sugar

2 large eggs

2/3 c skim milk

1/3 c water

3/4 t vanilla extract or almond extract or your favorite liqueur

2 T melted butter to coat the pan

Fresh strawberries, mixed berries or caramelized brown sugar and cinnamon apples

Whipped cream or cool whip

Maple syrup

Sift the flour into a bowl. Re-sift with the salt, baking powder, and powdered sugar.

In a separate bowl, beat the eggs. Add the milk, water, and vanilla. Beat again. Stir in the flour mixture until well mixed.

In a greased heated skillet, add about 1/2 cup of the batter and rotate the pan in the air to thoroughly coat the bottom. Cook until light golden brown and flip. Cook until light golden brown. Serve with desired toppings.

Broccoli & Ham Quiche

My sister gave me this recipe for a dynamite low calorie quiche. I actually made this for her wedding brunch, along with Quiche Lorraine.

9" pie crust (made from scratch or store bought) and a pie plate

16 oz egg whites

2 eggs with yolks

1/2 c skim milk

1/2 t salt

1/2 t pepper

4 strips bacon, cooked and chopped

1/2 white onion thinly sliced and cooked in bacon grease until translucent

1/2 c cooked ham, diced

1/2 c cheddar cheese, shredded

2 c frozen broccoli, thawed and diced

Make sure to poke pie crust with fork to reduce bubbling or use pie weights. Bake crust at 400 degrees for 10 minutes.

Add onions to bottom of pie crust. Mix the rest of the ingredients together, except for cheddar cheese and bacon. Pour over onions. Top with cheese and bacon.

Bake at 350 degrees, for 25 minutes or until cooked through.

Huevos Rancheros

1 28 oz can whole peeled tomatoes, undrained

1/4 c fresh cilantro, chopped

1/2 c yellow onion, chopped

3 cloves garlic

1 large jalapeño (seeded if desired)

1 t kosher salt

Mix all ingredients in a food processor, until mostly blended. Set aside.

1 lb chorizo sausage (Brown sausage in pan. Add sauce from food processor. Simmer for 20 minutes. Best to let marinate overnight in the fridge.)

1 can refried beans, heated (or black beans)

2 avocados, sliced

Cilantro for garnish

Shredded Mexican cheese or Monterey Jack cheese

Sour cream

Poached eggs, cooked over easy (or your favorite prepared eggs)

Crispy corn flat tortillas

Spread tortilla with refried beans. Layer with egg and sauce. Garnish with desired toppings.

Quiche Lorraine

This is fantastic brunch dish and it is easy to make in a large chaffing dish for large parties. I made this for my sister's after wedding brunch. People could not get enough. Pair with a make your own bloody or mimosa bar. Serve with a big salad and a bowl of fresh cut seasonal fruit.

9" pie crust (made from scratch or store bought) and a pie plate

5 strips bacon, cooked and chopped

1 yellow onion, thinly sliced and cooked in bacon grease until translucent

1/2 c Gruyere, cubed

1/2 c Swiss cheese, shredded

4 eggs, beaten lightly

1 c heavy cream

1 c skim milk

1/4 t nutmeg

1/2 t salt

1/4 t fresh ground black pepper

Make sure to poke pie crust with fork to reduce bubbling or use pie weights. Bake crust at 400 degrees for 10 minutes.

Add onions to bottom of pie crust. Mix the rest of the ingredients together and pour in pie crust over onions.

Bake at 350 degrees, for 25 minutes or until cooked through.

Waffles

My family grew up on waffles. My mother made waffles for breakfast more than any other breakfast dish.

Waffle maker, with oil or butter to coat to prevent waffles from sticking

1 1/2 c all-purpose flour

5 T powdered buttermilk

1/2 t baking powder

1/2 t baking soda

1 c skim milk

1/4 c heavy cream

2 large eggs

1/4 c good quality butter, melted

In a bowl, mix dry ingredients together.

Separate the eggs into two bowls.

In another bowl, whip the cream. Add the milk, egg yolks, and butter to the cream.

Combine and stir mixtures together, except the egg whites.

Whip the egg whites until soft peaks form. Fold the egg whites into the main mixture.

Use waffle maker to make waffles. Top with fresh berries, fresh whipped cream or cool whip, and syrup.

My Mom's Granola

My mother made this granola recipe for as long as I can remember. I remember she made pans and pans of it and stored it in old coffee tins for my sister and me to have before or after school.

2 C Quaker Old Fashioned Oats

1/2 c sliced almonds

1 c raw wheat germ

1/3 c cold pressed safflower oil

1/2 c real honey

Combine oats, almonds, and wheat germ. Drizzle liquid on dry ingredients on a cookie sheet. Cook slowly in the oven at 225 degrees for 1 hour, stirring every 15 minutes. After 1 hour, turn the oven off and let cool before removing from oven.

Serve in a bowl with milk or as a yogurt topping.

Store in air tight container once fully cooled.

Pasta & Sauces

My Lasagna

This is my godson and goddaughter's favorite dish that I make.

1 lb spicy Italian sausage

1 1/2 lb lean ground beef

1 white onion, chopped finely

3 cloves garlic, minced

1 28 oz can diced tomatoes

2 6 oz cans tomato paste

1 8 oz can of tomato sauce

1 8 oz can of oregano basil tomato sauce

1/2 c water

4 fresh or dried bay leaves

2 T fennel seeds

5 T Italian seasoning

1/2 t cayenne pepper

1 T salt

1 t fresh ground black pepper

5 T fresh parsley, chopped

30 oz part skim ricotta

2 large eggs

1 lb mozzarella cheese, shredded

1 lb parmesan cheese, grated

14 lasagna noodles

1 t salt

Directions for My Lasagna

In a Dutch oven, combine the sausage, beef, onion, and garlic. Cook and stir until browned. Thoroughly stir in tomato paste. Add the diced tomatoes, both cans of tomato sauce, water, bay leaves, fennel, Italian seasoning, cayenne, 1T salt, fresh ground black pepper, and 2 T of parsley. Stir. Simmer covered on medium low heat for 2 hours, stirring occasionally. Taste test and add more seasonings if need be.

In a large mixing bowl, combine the ricotta, eggs, 1/2 t salt, and 3 T remaining parsley. Mix well and set aside.

In a large stock pot, bring water to a boil for lasagna noodles. Once boiling, add 1 T salt and noodles. Cook until noodles are al dente. Remove from heat. Reserve 1/4 cup of the pasta water and stir into the sauce. Drain and rinse the noodles in cold water.

In a 12" x 15" lasagna pan, add enough sauce to cover the bottom. Add 7 noodles in a single layer. Spread half the ricotta mixture evenly on top of the noodles. Sprinkle with one-third of the parmesan and one-third of the mozzarella. Repeat. Finish with mozzarella and parmesan cheese.

Bake at 350 degrees for 45-60 minutes or until top is golden brown. Let stand for 10 minutes before cutting. Serve with garlic bread, fresh parmesan cheese, and a caesar salad.

Vegetable Lasagne

This is a delicious recipe we have had with our very good friends, the Sweatt's, at the Sweatt Ranch in Evergreen, CO.

1 lb spicy ground sausage

9 lasagna noodles, cooked al dente

1/3 c parmesan cheese, grated

3/4 c Fontina cheese

4 shallots, peeled and chopped

2 lb yellow and green summer squash, cut into 1/2" pieces

Extra virgin olive oil

Salt and pepper

2 c cherry tomatoes, cut in half

1/2 c fresh basil, chopped

2 T fresh chives, chopped

2 t fresh garlic, minced

3 1/2 c vegetable broth

5 T all-purpose flour

1/4 c heavy whipping cream

1 1/2 T Dijon mustard

1 egg, beaten

Directions for Vegetable Lasagna

Preheat oven to 450 degrees.

Preheat a baking sheet.

In a sauté pan, brown the sausage. Drain. Set aside.

In a large mixing bowl, combine shallots, squash, olive oil, salt and pepper. Toss lightly. Place on single layer on preheated baking sheet. Bake for 10-15 minutes, or until very lightly browned. Set aside.

Turn oven to broil on high.

In a roasting pan, place tomatoes in a single layer. Broil on high for 5-10 minutes, or until tomatoes begin to bubble. Set aside.

Turn oven to 350 degrees.

In a large mixing bowl, add the vegetable mixture and tomatoes. Add chives, garlic, and 1/4 c basil. Toss lightly.

In a small bowl, combine flour and broth. Whisk ingredients together until well blended.

In a small sauce pan over medium heat, add oil. Add the broth mixture. Add the whipping cream, mustard, salt and pepper. Cook for 3-5 minutes, stirring occasionally, until sauce begins to thicken. Remove from heat.

In a small bowl, add the egg. Beat slightly. Slowly add the broth mixture to the egg while stirring.

To assemble, take half the sauce and spread on the bottom of a 13" x 9" lasagna pan. Place 3 noodles in a single layer over the sauce. Add the veggies in a single layer. Add another layer of noodles. Add the sausage in a single layer. Add the final layer of noodles. Top with the remaining sauce and cheese. Bake at 350 until cheese is golden brown. Let stand for 10 minutes before cutting.

My Mom's Lasagna

One of my absolute favorite dinners growing up.

2 1/2 34 oz jars of Traditional Prego Pasta Sauce

24 oz cottage cheese (or ricotta)

1/2 t salt

1/4 t oregano

1/4 c parmesan cheese, grated

3/4 lb mozzarella, shredded

1 1/2 lb Italian sausage (spicy or mild)

1/3 lb ground beef

1 lb lasagna noodles, cooked al dente and drained

In a mixing bowl, mix the cottage cheese, salt, oregano, and parmesan cheese. Set aside.

In a sauté pan, brown the sausage and beef. Drain.

In a 12" x 15" lasagna pan, add 3 T of water and enough sauce to make a layer on the bottom of the pan. Place half the lasagna noodles on top of the sauce in a single layer. Take half the cheese mixture and spread it on top of the noodles. Repeat. Finish with mozzarella cheese.

Bake at 350 degrees for 45 -60 minutes, or until edges are golden brown. Remove from oven and let rest for 10 minutes before cutting.

Tuna Noodle Casserole

This is a great dish that will warm you up on a cool night. It also makes great leftovers, hot or cold. Don't forget to give the tuna juice to your kitty. I remember our family cat, Oreo, would come running into the kitchen with the sound of a can opener opening a can, hoping it was tuna juice.

2 10.5 oz cans cream of mushroom soup

2 5 oz cans white albacore tuna in water (or 2 chicken breasts or canned chicken)

1/2 c sweet peas (optional)

5 c extra wide egg noodles

1 c chow mein noodles (or fried onions)

1/2 c milk

Salt and pepper to taste

Bring a pot of water to a boil. Add egg noodles and cook until al dente. Drain.

In a casserole dish, add the cream of mushroom soup, milk, salt and pepper. Mix well. Stir in drained tuna and peas. Stir in egg noodles. Top with chow mein noodles or fried onions.

Bake at 350 degrees for 25-30 minutes, until edges are light golden brown or until heated through.

Chicken & Basil Pasta Salad

This is a light and fun dish in the summer. Can be served hot or cold.

1/2 box bowtie pasta (or your favorite pasta)

2 chicken breasts (or shrimp)

Greek seasoning (or salt and pepper)

Extra virgin olive oil

2 t milk

2 t heavy whipping cream

1 c yellow zucchini, sliced

1 c green zucchini, sliced

1 heirloom tomato, cut into bite sized chunks (or any fresh in season tomatoes)

1 c frozen or fresh peas (fresh is better)

1/4 c fresh basil, plus more for garnish

1 lemon

1 1/2 t garlic, minced

Pecorino Romano cheese, grated

1/2 t garlic salt

Fresh ground black pepper

Sea salt

Directions for Chicken & Basil Pasta Salad

Bring a pot of water to a boil. Salt the water and add the pasta. Cook until al dente. Drain the pasta and rinse with cold water to stop the cooking. Place pasta in large mixing bowl. Set aside.

Season the chicken with Greek seasoning and grill. Cut into cubes or strips. Set aside.

In a sauté pan, over medium heat, add the oil, garlic, and a little fresh ground black pepper. Stir and cook for 1 minute. Add the juice of 1 lemon, but save the rind to zest pasta before serving. Add the milk, heavy cream, and basil. Cook for 2 minutes, stirring occasionally. Remove from heat. Set aside.

In another sauté pan, over medium heat, add some oil, garlic salt, fresh ground black pepper, peas, and zucchini. Cook for 3-4 minutes, stirring occasionally until vegetables are cooked to your liking. Toss in the tomatoes. Stir. Cook for another 2 minutes. Remove from heat.

Add the veggies and the chicken to the pasta. Toss lightly. Add the lemon and garlic sauce and roughly 3 T of grated cheese. Toss lightly.

Top with fresh basil, lemon zest, and grated cheese. Serve with a crostini.

Pasta with Chicken and Vegetables

This is a great dish for summer. You can make this with as many of your favorite fresh vegetables as you like.

12 oz Ronzoni Super Greens Thin Spaghetti, cooked al dente

3 chicken breasts, cubed into 1" pieces

1 yellow zucchini, sliced

1 green zucchini, sliced

1/2 c cherry red tomatoes

2 c broccoli florets

4 oz Baby Bella mushrooms, sliced

4 cloves garlic, sliced thin

1/2 c dry white wine

2 chicken bouillon cubes

1 c pasta water

1/2 t fresh ground black pepper

1 t red pepper flakes

2 t oregano

1 t garlic salt

1 T extra virgin olive oil

1/2 c Pecorino Romano cheese, grated, plus more for serving

Directions for Pasta with Chicken & Vegetables

Cook pasta until al dente. Drain and reserve 1 cup of the pasta water.

In a large skillet over medium-high heat, add the extra virgin olive oil, pasta water, bouillon cubes, red pepper flakes, chicken, pepper, and oregano. Cook until chicken is almost cooked through. Add the white wine and bring to a boil. Add vegetables, and garlic salt. Stir and continue to cook until vegetables are cooked through and most of the liquid has evaporated. Stir in spaghetti and cheese. Top with grated cheese.

Breads

Popovers

Popover pan

2 eggs, at room temperature

1 c 2% milk, at room temperature

1 c all-purpose flour, at room temperature

1/2 t salt

4 T butter

Heat oven to 450 degrees. Mix the eggs, milk, flour, and salt in a mixing bowl.

Grease popover pan with butter and place a small piece of butter in each cup. Place in oven for 5 minutes or until butter is bubbly. Fill each cup just over half way with batter. Bake 20 minutes, until golden brown.

Serve with marmalade or butter.

Tip: Do not open the oven while the popovers are baking or they may fall.

Delicious Banana Bread

1/2 c quality butter

1 c white sugar

2 eggs

1 1/2 t vanilla extract (or lemon juice)

1 3/4 c all-purpose flour

1 t baking soda

1/2 t salt

1/2 c sour cream

1/2 c chopped walnuts

3 bananas, very brown and ripe

1/2 t ground cloves

1/2 t cinnamon

In a KitchenAid Stand Mixer, mix sugar and butter until creamy. Add eggs and vanilla and mix well. In another bowl, sift the flour, baking soda, and salt. Add to batter. Mix well. Fold in ground cloves, cinnamon, sour cream, bananas, and walnuts.

Butter a loaf pan. Pour batter into pan and bake at 350 degrees for 45 minutes or until edges are pulling away from pan and a toothpick comes out clean.

Use a spatula when done and release the bread from the pan. Flip over and let cool on wire rack or cutting board.

Banana Muffins with Streusel

1/2 c quality butter

1 c white sugar

2 eggs

1 1/2 t vanilla extract (or lemon juice)

1 3/4 c all-purpose flour

1 t baking soda

1/2 t salt

1/2 c sour cream

1/2 c chopped walnuts

3 bananas, very brown and ripe

1/2 t ground cloves

1/2 t cinnamon

Streusel topping ingredients

2/3 c brown sugar, packed

1/4 c all-purpose flour

1/2 t ground cinnamon

3 T butter

Directions for Banana Muffins with Streusel

In a KitchenAid Stand Mixer, mix sugar and butter until creamy. Add eggs and vanilla and mix well. In another bowl, sift the flour, baking soda and salt. Add to batter. Mix well. Fold in ground cloves, cinnamon, sour cream and bananas.

In a small bowl, combine the streusel ingredients and stir well.

Butter a muffin pan well or use liners. Fill cups 2/3 full with batter. Sprinkle with streusel topping. Bake at 350 degrees for 15-20 minutes, until a toothpick comes out clean.

Kolache

This Paulaha Czechoslovakian Sweet Bread was passed down in my family for generations.

Dough

3/4 c half and half

1/2 c sugar

1 t salt

1/2 c butter

4 t vanilla

1/3 c warm water (between 105-115 F)

2 packages active dry yeast

3 eggs, at room temperature

5 1/2 - 6 1/2 c all-purpose flour

Crisco

While dough is rising, make the filling.

Filling ingredients

2 c walnuts, crushed in a blender

1/2 c sugar

1/2 c brown sugar

1/4 c butter

1 t vanilla

1/3 c half and half

Directions for Kolache

Dough

Scald the half and half in a pan over medium heat. Stir in the butter until it is melted. Add sugar and salt and stir. Cool to lukewarm (115 F degrees).

In a warmed KitchenAid Stand Mixer bowl, add the warm water and yeast. Stir until dissolved. Add lukewarm half and half mixture, eggs, and 5 c of flour. Attach bowl and dough hook. Turn to speed 2 and mix for 2 minutes. Continue on speed 2 and add remaining flour, 1/2 c at a time, until dough clings to hook and sides of bowl are clean; roughly 5 minutes. Knead on speed 2 for an additional 7-10 minutes or until dough is smooth and elastic.

Place dough in a Crisco greased bowl, turning to grease all the dough. Cover with a damp flour sack towel. Let rise in a warm place free from draft for about 1 hour, or until dough has doubled in size. Punch dough down. Cut dough into 4 equal sections and place damp towel back over bowl.

Filling

In a bowl, combine the crushed walnuts, sugar and brown sugar. Set aside.

Scald the half and half in a pan over medium heat. Stir in the butter and vanilla. Pour over the nuts. Stir together. Set filling aside.

To assemble and bake

Take one quarter of the dough and roll it out thin (about 1/4" thick) to make a rectangle. Spread a thin layer of the filling on the dough, but make sure the filling does not reach the edges. (You need the edges to seal the dough.) Roll it up and pinch to seal the filling in the roll. A little milk spread on the edge helps seal the roll. Bake on a parchment-lined sheet pan at 375 F for about 25 minutes, or until lightly browned.

Crostini for Soups & Salads

1/2 loaf ciabatta bread, sliced thin

1/2 c extra virgin olive oil

1/2 t garlic salt

2/3 c Pecorino Romano cheese, grated

I find if the bread is somewhat frozen, it is much easier to slice 1/4" slices.

In a small dish combine the oil and garlic salt. Using a pastry or basting brush, brush both sides of the bread lightly with the oil mixture. Place in a single layer on a cookie sheet. Bake at 350 degrees until bottom side is light golden brown. Flip and top with grated cheese. Bake for another 5-10 minutes, or until light golden brown on both sides. Once cooled, store in an airtight container.

Dough Boys

Growing up, each time my mother made homemade bread, my sister and I would request Dough Boys. They basically taste like doughnuts from the Minnesota State Fair.

Bread dough (French or sourdough)

3 c safflower oil

1/2 c sugar

1 T cinnamon

In a bowl, combine sugar and cinnamon. Set aside.

In a small pot, bring the oil to medium heat.

Flatten the bread dough; about 1" thick. Cut into 6" x 3" pieces. On one of the longer sides, cut 4-5 slits (about half way through to the other side). Drop in heated oil and fry until golden brown. Flip and cook until other side is also golden brown. Remove and place on paper towel. While still warm, roll in sugar mixture. Serve warm.

Soups
& Stews
& Sauces

Chicken & Dumplings

My mom made this dish for us on special occasions or after school on chilly days. It is truly one of my favorites. The house always smells amazing when you cook this.

6 chicken breasts (frozen or thawed)

2 large white onions, chopped

5 stalks celery, chopped in 1/2" pieces

6 large carrots, chopped in 1/2" discs

3 fresh or dried bay leaves

1 t fresh ground black pepper

6 c water

6 chicken bouillon cubes

1 t mace

Dumpling ingredients

Bisquick, parsley, salt, and milk

Add all ingredients to a stock pot and bring to a boil. Simmer on low, covered, for about 2 hours.

Once chicken and vegetables are cooked to your liking, it is time to make the dumplings. In a large mixing bowl, add about 4 cups Bisquick, some parsley for color, and a couple dashes of salt. Add enough milk to make a sticky, but not runny, dumpling consistency. Spoon the dumpling batter on top of chicken to cover what is in the pot. Cover and cook on low for about 10 minutes, or until dumplings are cooked through. Let rest covered for 10 minutes. Then serve.

Spicy Lemon Aioli

Great sauce for crab cakes or paninis.

9 T dijon mustard

1 c honey

2 1/2 c mayonnaise

4 T habanero, minced

1/3 mango (optional)

2 T garlic, minced

2 T fresh lemon juice

1/8 t cayenne pepper

In a glass bowl, combine all ingredients and mix well. Cover and let sit overnight in the refrigerator to let the flavors mix.

Cream of Zucchini Soup

I received this delicious recipe from my brother-in-law's family - the Schwartz family. It is a great first course, especially before fish.

3 T butter

3 medium (or two large) sweet onions, thinly sliced

2 cloves garlic, minced (approximately 2 heaping teaspoons)

26 oz chicken broth (I use College Inn low fat / low sodium)

4 medium zucchini, thinly sliced

2 stalks of celery with leaves, thinly sliced

1 T parsley, chopped

1 t Kosher salt

1/2 t each of dried (jar) dill weed and dried (jar) basil leaves

1/4 t fresh ground black pepper

1 c 2% or whole milk (or half and half)

Grated parmesan cheese and lime slices for garnish

Directions for Cream of Zucchini Soup

Melt butter in skillet and sauté onions until tender, but not brown.

Add garlic and sauté for one minute.

Combine zucchini, celery, parsley, sautéed onion and garlic, spices, salt and pepper, and chicken broth in a large pot and stir.

Bring to a boil. Cover. Reduce heat and simmer for 30 minutes. Remove from heat. Let cool for 15 minutes.

Using either a food processor or a blender, puree mixture in small batches.

Strain pureed mixture through a sieve over a large bowl, pressing with a spoon (I do this because I like it smooth, but if you like it with more texture, you can skip this step).

When ready to serve, return to saucepan, add milk, and reheat.

Serve with grated parmesan cheese and lime slices, which are optional.

Chicken Tortilla Soup

1 yellow onion, chopped

2 T garlic

1 jalapeño, minced with seeds (or seedless)

Extra virgin olive oil

3 c cooked chicken, shredded

1 28 oz can crushed tomatoes

3 c chicken broth

1 15 oz can Bush's Black Beans (in sauce)

2 4 oz cans green chillies, diced

1 lime, juiced

1 14.5 oz can corn

2 T chili powder

1 t ground cumin

1/2 t oregano

1/2 t cayenne pepper

1/4 fresh cilantro, chopped

Tortilla chips, jalapeños, avocado, fresh cilantro, Monterey Jack cheese, and sour cream for topping.

Directions for Chicken Tortilla Soup

In a large dutch oven on medium heat, add the onion, garlic, jalapeño, and olive oil. Cook and stir occasionally until the onions are soft. Stir in the chili powder, cumin, oregano, and cayenne. Stir in the crushed tomatoes, green chillies, lime juice, and broth. Simmer for 15 minutes, stirring occasionally.

Stir in the chicken, beans, corn, and cilantro. Bring to a boil, then simmer on low for at least an hour. Taste test and add any additional seasonings.

Garnish with desired toppings.

Beef Stew

1 lb bacon, sliced

2 1/2 lb beef, cubed into 1" pieces

3/4 c Wondra flour

2 t onion powder

2 t garlic salt

3 t fresh ground black pepper

2 leeks, cleaned and minced

2 white onions, chopped finely

3 T butter

4 fresh or dried bay leaves

3 cloves garlic, minced

2 jalapeño peppers, minced

2 T thyme

2 T rosemary

1/4 c parsley, chopped

1 c red wine (not sweet)

6 c water

6 beef bouillon cubes

6 small red potatoes, rinsed and cut into 1" cubes

5 medium carrots, peeled and cut into 1" pieces

3 stalks celery, rinsed and cut into 1" pieces

2 large Portobello mushrooms, cut into 2" pieces

1 t corn starch

Crusty ciabatta bread, garlic bread, or crostini

Directions for Beef Stew

In a mixing bowl, combine and mix together the Wondra flour, onion powder, garlic salt, and 2 t black pepper. Dust the beef cubes in the flour mixture. Set aside.

In a large Dutch oven on medium, add the bacon and cook until bacon is done. Remove and chop. Brown the beef in the bacon grease in the pot. Remove.

Add the leeks, onion, and butter to the Dutch oven on medium heat. Cook until the leeks and onions are lightly browned. Add the bacon and beef back into the pot. Add the bay leaves, garlic, jalapeño peppers, thyme, rosemary, parsley, and 1 t black pepper. Pour in the red wine and scrape the bottom of the pan with a wooden spoon. Let cook for 5 minutes. Add 3 c water and 3 beef bouillon cubes. Simmer for 1 hour.

Add the potatoes, carrots, celery, mushrooms, 3 cups water, 3 bouillon cubes, and corn starch. Simmer for 1-2 more hours. Serve with crusty ciabatta bread, garlic bread, or crostini.

White Chicken Chili

This is a twist on a chili recipe friends shared with me.

1 Rotisserie chicken, skin removed and shredded (or 5 chicken breasts cooked and shredded)

2 T extra virgin olive oil

2 large yellow onions, finely chopped

2 jalapeños, minced with seeds

5 cloves garlic, minced

2 15 oz cans Bush's Great Northern White Chili Beans in Mild Chili Sauce

1 15 oz can Bush's Cannelloni Beans

2 4 oz can green chillies, diced

1 14.5 oz can corn

1 32 oz box chicken broth

1 32 oz box chicken stock

2 t oregano

2 t ground cumin

1/2 t cayenne pepper

8 oz Monterey Jack cheese, shredded

Fritos Original Corn Chips, jalapeños, and sour cream for topping

Directions for White Chicken Chili

In a Dutch oven over medium high heat, cook the onions in oil for about 5 minutes, stirring frequently, until translucent.

Add all the other ingredients, except the shredded cheese and toppings. Bring to a boil and simmer for 2 hours. Add the shredded cheese and cook until cheese is dissolved. Serve with Fritos Original Corn Chips, sour cream, and diced jalapeños.

Chili

2 1/2 lb lean ground beef

1 lb spicy Italian sausage

4 slices bacon, cooked and chopped

2 small yellow onions, chopped

3 stalks celery, chopped

1/2 c yellow bell pepper, chopped

1/2 c red bell pepper, chopped

1/2 c green bell pepper, chopped

3 jalapeños, minced

4 beef bouillon cubes

1/2 beer

5 T chili powder

1/2 t cayenne pepper

1 T Worcestershire sauce

4 cloves garlic, mined

1 T ground cumin

1 T oregano

1 t basil

1 t fresh ground black pepper

1 t salt

2 16 oz cans Bush's Chili Beans in Mild Sauce

2 16 oz cans Bush's Chili Beans in Spicy Sauce

2 28 oz cans diced tomatoes, undrained

1 6 oz can tomato paste

Directions for Chili

In a large Dutch oven over medium heat, combine the beef, sausage, and onion. Cook until browned. Stir in the tomato paste. Add remaining ingredients. Simmer for 3 hours, stirring occasionally. Top with green onions, cheddar cheese, sour cream, minced Jalapeños, and Fritos Original Corn Chips.

Brown Family Spaghetti Sauce

2 lb ground beef

5 hot Italian sausages (or mild)

1 6 oz can tomato paste

1 white onion, diced

3 cloves garlic, minced

2 29 oz cans tomato sauce

1 24 oz jar Traditional Prego Pasta Sauce (or any flavor preference)

3 fresh bay leaves (or dried)

1 T Italian herbs

1/4 c extra virgin olive oil

1/2 t garlic salt

1 T fresh parsley, chopped

In a large Dutch oven on medium, brown the sausages. Remove the sausages and place on a paper towel. Add the ground beef, onion, and garlic. Cook until browned. Thoroughly mix in the tomato paste. Add and stir in the rest of the ingredients, including the sausages. Bring to a boil and simmer at least 4 hours. Serve over your favorite pasta and garlic bread.

Meat
& Poultry
& Sea

Slow Cooked BBQ Brisket Sandwiches

6 lb brisket

Brioche buns

1/2 c extra virgin olive oil

Seasoning

1 T garlic salt

1 T salt

1 T paprika

2 t onion powder

2 t fresh ground black pepper

1 t ground cumin

1 t cayenne pepper

BBQ Sauce

2 1/2 c spicy BBQ sauce (Rufus Teague Touch O' Heat is great)

4 cloves garlic, minced

2 T brown sugar

Directions for Slow Cooked BBQ Brisket Sandwiches

Let the brisket sit until it comes to room temperature. Thoroughly rub brisket with oil. Combine seasoning ingredients and rub generously over the entire brisket. Place brisket fat side up in slow cooker.

In a bowl, combine the sauce ingredients and pour over the brisket.

Place brisket, fat side up, in slow cooker and cook on high for one hour. Flip and baste and cook on high for another hour. Flip again and drop temperature to low. Cook another 3-5 hours, until brisket is tender and starts to fall apart. Pull from slow cooker and let rest for 15 minutes. Slice across the grain. Top with drippings, BBQ sauce, fried onions, and sliced pickles.

Grilled Pheasant Skewers

My husband goes pheasant hunting every year. This is the recipe we make with the pheasant he brings home. It makes a great appetizer. My sister's dog, Bear, also loves these (minus the jalapeño peppers, of course).

1 pheasant, defrosted and cleaned

1 lb bacon

1 12 oz jar sliced jalapeño peppers

Cut the pheasant into 2" pieces. Put the pieces in a bowl. Pour the liquid from the jalapeño peppers over the pheasant. Stir. Let marinate for 30 minutes. You can also soak the pheasant in buttermilk overnight to reduce the gamey taste.

Put a jalapeño pepper on each piece of pheasant. Wrap with a 1/2 slice of bacon and secure on a skewer.

Grill on medium high heat until bacon is crisp and the pheasant is cooked through.

Serve with ranch or BBQ sauce.

Beer Can Chicken

1 whole chicken, defrosted, rinsed, and patted dry

Safflower oil

1 can beer, opened

Beer can chicken stand (optional)

Salt

Fresh ground black pepper

2 t garlic salt

2 t oregano

2 t ground ginger

2 t onion powder

1 t paprika

1/2 t cayenne pepper

Rinse the chicken thoroughly and pat dry. Thoroughly rub with safflower oil.

Mix all seasonings together in a small bowl, with 1 t salt and 1 t pepper. Rub seasoning all over chicken and under skin. Salt and pepper the cavity as well. Drink or discard roughly a third of the beer, so it does not overflow.

Place chicken cavity over the beer can or place the chicken on a beer-can rack with the beer can placed in the holder on the rack. Grill on indirect medium heat until chicken reaches 165 degrees. You can also bake in a 350 degree oven.

Parmesan Chicken

4 skinless and boneless chicken breasts

4 T melted butter

1/4 c parmesan cheese, grated

1/2 t fresh parsley, chopped

Rinse chicken and pat dry.

Preheat oven to 350 degrees.

On a plate, mix the parmesan cheese and parsley.

On another plate, melt the butter.

Roll the chicken in the butter, then roll it in the cheese mixture. Place on baking sheet and bake for 35 minutes or until chicken is fully cooked through and the parmesan cheese is golden brown.

Hot Beef Italian Sandwiches

Eye of round steak (roughly 7 1/2 pounds)

3 fresh or dried bay leaves

8 c water

5 beef bouillon cubes

2 t fresh ground black pepper

2 t dried oregano

1 t dried basil

2 t onion powder

2 t fresh parsley, chopped

2 t garlic salt

3 Good Seasons .7 oz Dry Italian Salad Dressing packets

Provolone or Swiss cheese slices

Hot peppers

Crusty buttered ciabatta rolls

In a Dutch oven, combine the beef, bay leaves, water, bouillon cubes, black pepper, oregano, basil, onion powder, parsley, garlic salt, and dressing packets. Bring to a boil. Simmer covered for 4 hours or until it can be shredded with a fork. (Add more water if necessary.) Serve with buttered crusty rolls, cheese, and hot peppers.

If a slow cooker is used instead of a Dutch oven, use 5 c water. Cook on low for 10 to 12 hours or on high for 4 to 6 hours, until meat can be shredded with a fork.

Basil Garlic Salmon

2 8 oz salmon fillets, skin on or skin off

2 T extra virgin olive oil

2 T garlic, minced

2 T basil, chopped

Fresh ground back pepper

Lemon

Place the salmon fillets in a casserole dish. Smear the garlic on top of the fillets. Drizzle with olive oil. Add the basil and a few grinds of pepper. Slice the lemon thin and place a couple slices on top of each fillet.

Bake at 350 degrees for 15-20 minutes, until the fish flakes easily with a fork at its thickest point. (Personal preferences do vary with salmon, as they do with steak, so you may want to cook it a little more or less.) Serve with steamed broccoli.

Rosemary & Garlic Lamb Chops

Lamb rack

5 garlic cloves, minced

3 T extra virgin olive oil

2 T fresh rosemary

1 t fresh ground black pepper

Horseradish sauce for dipping (optional)

In a small bowl, combine all the ingredients. Then smear over the chops. Marinate in a sealed plastic bag for at least one hour or overnight.

Grill on indirect medium high heat until desired temp is reached (130 degrees is recommended for medium). Low and slow is the best way to cook the lamb. Cut each chop and serve with horseradish sauce.

Pork Carnitas

Definitely a crowd pleaser. I make this year round. Great to use in poutine. Freezes well.

8 lb pork butt, cut into fist sized pieces

1/4 c vegetable oil

3 T kosher salt

3 T fresh ground black pepper

1 1/2 white onion, chopped

1 large head of garlic, minced

6 T fresh lime juice

3 T chili powder

2 t dried oregano

2 t ground cumin

5 c chicken broth (or 5 c water and 5 chicken bouillon cubes)

1/2 t cayenne pepper

Heat oil in a Dutch oven. Salt and pepper pork butt pieces. Brown a few pieces at a time in oil, then add everything back in. Simmer three hours. Transfer pieces to baking sheet and shred with fork. Drizzle broth from the Dutch oven over shredded pork. Bake at 350 degrees, until lightly browned.

Serve with warm corn or flour tortillas, fresh cilantro, chopped red onion, sliced avocado, sour cream, Monterey Jack cheese, and hot sauce.

Cornish Game Hens

My mother always made the best Cornish game hens. We had them quite often, especially on special occasions. I remember my sister and I felt lucky when my parent's gave us the crispy skin from their game hens. Over the years, I have added a little twist on the recipe to make a balanced meal.

4 Cornish game hens (normally one per person), fully defrosted, rinsed, and at room temp

Safflower oil

Salt and fresh ground black pepper

Cayenne pepper

Italian herbs (or your favorite herbs)

3 c water

3 chicken bouillon cubes

8-10 baby red potatoes, washed and poked

5-7 whole carrots, peeled

2 white onions, chopped

In a casserole dish, assemble the potatoes, carrots, and onions. Add the water and bouillon cubes. Sprinkle with Italian herbs and some fresh-ground black pepper.

Rinse and dry the hens thoroughly. Thoroughly rub the hens with safflower oil. Salt and pepper the cavity and the entire hen. Sprinkle the breasts with a little cayenne. Place the hens breast side up on top of the veggies in the casserole dish. Bake at 325 degrees, for 90-120 minutes or until the juices run clear and the skin is crispy brown.

Leg of Lamb

My family enjoys this grilled leg of lamb each Easter at our home.

Leg of lamb - bone in - roughly 11 lb (can do boneless)

1/4 c fresh rosemary, chopped

1/4 c fresh thyme, chopped and 4 sprigs fresh rosemary

1/4 c fresh oregano, chopped

2 t salt

1 t fresh ground black pepper

2 lemons

5 heads of garlic, tops cut off

Extra virgin olive oil

In a small bowl, combine the chopped herbs, lemon zest from lemons (hold on to the lemons), salt, and black pepper. Mix. Rub evenly and thoroughly on leg of lamb. Put leg of lamb in a large plastic bag and let marinate overnight (or as long as 2 days).

In a large skillet or wok over medium heat, add the extra virgin olive oil. Add the leg of lamb. Keep turning and flipping until the leg is thoroughly browned on all sides. Roughly 30 minutes. Place leg of lamb, bone down, in a grill-safe pan with the sprigs of rosemary on top. Cut the lemons in half. Wedge the lemons and garlic around the lamb. Preheat grill. Put lamb on indirect heat on grill. Turn temp down to medium low and cook for about 90 minutes or until temp near bone reaches 140 degrees (for medium rare) or until desired temp is reached. Let rest for 20 minutes before carving. Serve with heads of garlic.

Fall Off the Bone Slow Cooked Turkey

Fresh or fully thawed turkey, at room temperature (roughly 20 lb)

Salt

Fresh ground black pepper

Cayenne pepper

1 12 oz package Hormel salt pork

Safflower oil

Turkey Roaster

2 bags prepared Pepperidge Farm Sage & Onion Stuffing (or any other stuffing you prefer)

Rinse and thoroughly dry the turkey, removing all included giblets and neck. Rub bird thoroughly with safflower oil. Salt and pepper well, especially in the cavity. Stuff the turkey with the prepared stuffing until full. Any leftover stuffing can be placed in a casserole dish, covered with tin foil, and put in the fridge. Place the salt pork under the turkey. The salt pork not only flavors the turkey, it helps make an outstanding gravy. Place the turkey in the roaster, breast side up. Cook at 175 degrees overnight. If you plan to eat at 4 PM or 5 PM, my recommendation would be to put the turkey in the roaster no later than 10 PM the night before. When you wake in the morning, the home will smell heavenly. When I start preparing additional food for the dinner, probably around 3 PM, I put the remaining stuffing in the oven (covered in tin foil) at around 200 degrees until we are ready to pull the turkey. I recommend basting the turkey a few times. You can turn the turkey roaster up to 400 degrees for crispy skin 30-60 minutes prior to pulling the turkey. Or, you can use a butane torch. When the turkey is done, remove it from the roaster and immediately remove the stuffing. Place both stuffing batches in a serving bowl. Let the turkey rest for at least 15 minutes prior to carving.

BBQ Ribs

This is a great recipe for game days or summer nights. I typically serve the ribs with sautéed vegetables and macaroni and cheese.

Deep roasting pan

2 slabs ribs (your choice), at room temp

Salt

Pepper

Cayenne pepper

BBQ sauce

Heat oven to 275 degrees. Pat ribs dry with paper towels. Season ribs generously with salt and pepper on both sides. Sprinkle cayenne on both sides. Place ribs bone down in roasting pan and dome with aluminum foil. Cook for 2 hours. Remove from oven.

Cover ribs with your favorite BBQ sauce. Finish on grill on direct medium high heat until ends are slightly crispy or charred.

Spicy Tomato & Turkey Panini Sandwich

Slices of bread (I use sourdough and other breads)

Roasted turkey or oven roasted chicken breast, sliced thin

Slices of cheese (I use mozzarella and Swiss)

Fresh tomato, sliced

Red onion, sliced thin

Spinach

Spicy Lemon Aioli (or spicy mayonnaise)

Panini Press

Heat the panini press on medium.

Spread the aioli on the bread. Layer preferred meat, cheese, tomato slices, red onions, and spinach between two pieces of bread. Grill until cheese is melted and bread is toasted.

Turkey Panini Sandwich

Slices of bread (I use sourdough and other breads)

Roasted turkey or oven roasted chicken breast, sliced thin

Slices of mozzarella or Swiss cheese

Fresh tomato, sliced

Garlic salt

Panini Press

Heat the panini press on medium.

Sprinkle garlic salt on both sides of the tomato slices. Layer preferred meat, cheese, and tomato slices between two pieces of bread. Grill until cheese is melted and bread is toasted.

Sloppy Joes

This is an old time favorite. Serve with chips and a pickle.

1 lb lean ground beef

1/2 c white onion, roughly chopped

1/2 c green bell pepper, chopped

1 t yellow mustard or Grey Poupon

1 t garlic salt

1/2 t fresh ground black pepper

1/2 c ketchup

1/4 c spicy BBQ sauce

Brioche buns

Brown beef and onion in a Dutch oven over medium heat. Drain.

Add remaining ingredients and simmer for one hour, stirring occasionally. Serve on brioche buns.

Garlic Shrimp

If you love garlic, you will love this dish. I typically serve this with steamed broccoli or cauliflower rice.

1 lb shrimp, thawed, rinsed, peeled and deveined

3 T garlic, minced

1 T extra virgin olive oil or avocado oil

1 t Chef Paul Seafood Magic

1/4 t fresh ground black pepper

Heat a large skillet over medium heat. Add all ingredients and cook until shrimp are cooked through and water is nearly evaporated.

Desserts
& Sweets

Mom & Aunt Pam's Famous Caramel Corn

Hands down, my mom and Aunt Pam make the best caramel corn. Period.

6 quarts popcorn (remove all un-popped kernels). An air popper is best.

2 c brown sugar, packed firmly

1 c salted butter

1/2 c light corn syrup

1 t salt

1 t vanilla

3/4 t imitation butter flavoring

1 t baking soda

Nuts (optional) I like pecans

Spread popcorn on two cookie sheets. If you want to add nuts, sprinkle them on the popcorn before adding the syrup.

Syrup

Mix brown sugar, butter, corn syrup, and salt in a large heavy sauce pan. Bring to a full rolling boil. After boiling for a full 5 minutes, remove from heat. Stir in the vanilla and butter flavoring. Then add the baking soda. It will puff up. After it settles down, stir it again. Pour evenly on popcorn spread on two cookie sheets.

Place in oven preheated to 200 degrees and bake for one hour, stirring every 15 minutes. After one hour, remove from oven.

While still warm, pull apart into bite-size pieces or press into balls. Allow to completely cool. Store in air-tight containers.

Spritz Cookies

I have been making spritz cookies for as long as I can remember with my mom and sister. My favorite cookie press design is the long ruler one. It makes such a light and crispy cookie. To this day, this is still my favorite cookie. For fun or for special occasions, you can use food coloring to color the dough before putting in the press.

2 1/4 c all-purpose flour, sifted

3/4 c sugar

1/2 t salt

1/4 t baking powder

1 c good quality butter, cold (not melted or soft)

1 large egg

1 1/2 t vanilla (or almond extract)

Sprinkles

Spritz cookie press

Sift the flour, sugar, salt, and baking powder into a bowl.

In the mixing bowl for a KitchenAid Stand Mixer, cut the shortening into the dry ingredients with a pastry cutter or two knives until there are lots of small clumps. Add the egg and vanilla and beat with the KitchenAid white mixer spatula until mixed well. Chill for 10 minutes. Place dough in Spritz cookie press. Press cookies onto a non-stick cookie sheet or a cookie sheet lined with parchment paper. Decorate with sprinkles. Bake at 375 degrees until cookies are set. Store in air tight container or in freezer until ready to serve.

Dad's Favorite Apple Pie

2 pie crusts (from scratch or store bought) and a pie plate

1/2 c unsalted good quality butter

3 T all-purpose flour

1/4 c water

1/2 c brown sugar, packed

1/2 c sugar

1/4 t ground cinnamon

1/4 t nutmeg

1/4 t allspice

6 tart apples, such as Haralson

Peel, core, and slice apples. Set aside.

Preheat oven to 425 degrees.

In a sauce pan, melt the butter. Add the flour and stir to form a paste. Add the water, brown sugar, sugar, cinnamon, nutmeg, and allspice. Bring to a boil. Once a boil is reached, reduce heat and simmer on low for 3-5 minutes until sugar is dissolved. Remove from heat.

Place one pie crust in the pie plate and punch with fork to reduce the crust from bubbling. Add apples. Pour sugar mixture on top. Place second pie crust on top folding over and pinching the edges. Cut slits on top pie crust for venting. Place in a 425 degree oven for 15 minutes. Reduce temp to 350 and cook 45 minutes or until the apples are soft and crust is golden brown.

Scotch-A-Roos

My sister and I absolutely love these. I have never had a better recipe than this one.

1 c sugar

1 c Karo light corn syrup

1 cold fashioned creamy peanut butter (or crunchy)

6 c rice crispy cereal

1 1/4 c butterscotch chips

1 1/4 c semi-sweet chocolate chips

In a Dutch oven, over medium heat, mix together and heat the sugar and corn syrup. Heat until the mixture is nearly clear and lightly bubbling. Remove from heat and stir in the peanut butter. Add in the rice crispy cereal. Stir well to make sure cereal is well coated. Press evenly into a square or rectangle dish.

Combine the chips in a microwave safe bowl. Cook in microwave and stir frequently until chips are melted (roughly 2 minutes). Be careful to not over cook or burn the chocolate. Spread evenly on bars. Serve warm or cool.

Mom's S'More Pie

My mother wanted to make my sister and me a brand new dessert when we were little. She always had graham crackers on hand and decided to see what was in our pantry. She came up with this recipe. When my mom asked us what we should call it, we said "S'more Pie".

Crust

1 package original graham crackers

1 c sugar

1/2 cup butter, melted

Filling

1 5.9 oz package JELL-O Chocolate Fudge Instant Pudding (prepare as directed on box, with the 2 c milk)

8 oz marshmallows

2 T butter

4 oz regular cream cheese, whipped (better to whip yourself than to buy whipped cream cheese)

Crush graham crackers in bowl. Add melted butter and sugar. Mix. Press into pie plate as a crust. Reserve one T of crust mix to sprinkle on top.

In a dutch oven, melt 2 T butter. Add the marshmallows. Cook on low until marshmallows are melted. Remove from heat. Mix in the prepared pudding and cream cheese. Pour into pie crust. Sprinkle the reserved T of crust mix on top. Refrigerate until set. Roughly 3 hours.

Ginger Cookies

1 c shortening

1 c sugar

1 large egg

1 c dark molasses

2 T white vinegar

5 c all-purpose flour, sifted

1/2 t salt

1 1/2 t baking soda

2 T fresh ginger, grated

1 1/2 t cinnamon

1 1/2 t ground cloves

Cinnamon red imperials for decorating

White icing for decorating

In a bowl, sift dry ingredients. Set aside.

In a large mixing bowl or the mixing bowl for a KitchenAid Stand Mixer, cream the shortening and sugar using the KitchenAid white mixer spatula. Add the egg, molasses, vinegar, and ginger. Beat well. Slowly add in the dry ingredients. Chill for at least 5 hours or overnight. Roll. Cut. Decorate. Bake at 375 degrees until cookies are set. Keep an eye on the cookies, they bake much quicker than you think.

Grandma Gamelin's Chocolate Dessert

My mom's mother used to make this when she met her friends to play bridge.

1 3/4 c flour

3/4 c high quality butter

3/4 c walnuts, ground in coffee grinder or food processor

1 c regular Cool Whip

1 8 oz package of original cream cheese

1 c powdered sugar

2 5.9 oz package JELL-O Chocolate Fudge Instant Pudding

3 c milk (or chocolate milk)

Food processor or coffee grinder

Preheat oven to 350.

For crust, mix together the flour, butter, and walnuts in a food processor until finely blended. Press into a 9"X13" pan. Bake at 350 degrees for 25 minutes or until golden brown. Let cool.

In a bowl, mix the milk and pudding together. Spread on cooled crust.

In another bowl, whip the cream cheese. Add and whip in the cool whip, then the powdered sugar. Spread as top layer on the dessert. Chill in fridge. It is best if it can sit in the fridge overnight.

Scotch Shortbread

My mother always made this for our family. I remember she used to put the shortbread in a beautiful Warren Mackenzie pie dish about 2" thick. We would cut it up like a piece of pie. It was delicious, especially still warm from the oven.

1 1/2 c good quality butter

1 c powdered or granulated sugar

4 c all-purpose flour, sifted

Preheat oven to 300 degrees.

Cream butter until it is a consistency of whipped cream.

Gradually add in sugar. Beat until very light. Stir in the flour and knead until smooth. Press dough into pie plate and prick dough about a dozen times with a fork.

Bake until the edges are golden brown.

Date Bars

Filing

1 c sugar

1 c water

1 c dates

Crust

1 c Crisco shortening

1 c brown sugar

2 1/2 c Old Fashioned Oats

2 c all-purpose flour

1/2 t baking soda

1/4 t salt

3 T hot water, not boiling

Preheat oven to 350 degrees.

In a small dutch oven, over medium heat, cook the sugar, water, and dates until thickened. Roughly 20-25 minutes.

For the cookie base, cream the shortening. Add the sugar, oats, flour, baking soda, salt, and water. Mix thoroughly. Press 1/2 the mixture in bottom of pan.

Pour the filing evenly over the crust. Add remaining mixture on top. Bake for 30 minutes, or until top is slightly golden brown.

Strawberry Shortcake

2 1/2 c all-purpose baking mix, like Bisquick

2 T sugar

1 T lemon juice mixed with 1/2 c milk

3 T butter, melted

2 T corn starch

2 t water

1/2 t almond extract

1 T sliced almonds for topping (optional)

1 16 oz container of frozen sliced strawberries, with sugar added

2 c Cool Whip

Preheat oven to 350 degrees.

In a bowl, combine the Bisquick, sugar, lemon juice and milk mixture, melted butter, and almond extract. Stir only until soft dough forms. Drop 1/2 c drops on a sheet pan and bake until golden brown. Let cool. Break in half.

In a small bowl, stir together the corn starch and water. Set aside.

In a saucepan, over medium heat, heat strawberries until thawed. Add in the corn starch mixture and increase heat to high. Bring to a boil and boil for 1 minute, until thickened.

To assemble, take half a shortcake and top with Cool Whip. Place the other half on top and pour strawberries on top. Top with Cool Whip and almonds.

Paulaha Family Divinity

3 c sugar

3/4 c light corn syrup

1/2 c water

2 egg whites

1 t almond extract

1 c chopped walnuts

Place sugar, corn syrup, and water in a sauce pan. Over medium heat, cook to hard ball stage (248 F). Remove from heat and let stand until temperature reaches 220 F, WITHOUT STIRRING.

Using a KitchenAid Stand Mixer, place egg whites in a bowl and whip on speed 8 until soft peaks form. Gradually add syrup in a fine stream (takes about 3 minutes). Reduce to speed 4. Add extract and continue whipping 20-25 minutes or until mixture starts to become dry. Turn to stir speed and add chopped walnuts. Drop mixture from spoon onto wax or parchment paper.

Wedding Cakes

This recipe came from my Aunt Alice. The recipe card it is on is barely legible and is brittle and golden yellow.

1/2 c butter, creamed well

3 T powdered sugar

1 c all-purpose flour

1/2 c almonds, finely chopped

1 t vanilla

1/4 t salt

Preheat oven to 350 degrees.

Mix ingredients together well and roll into small round balls.

Bake on greased cookie sheet about 10 minutes or until very lightly browned on bottom.

Shake in a bag of powdered sugar while hot and again when cool.

A cheers…or a toast…

"Good food, good God, let's eat."

"Here's to us, who's like us, damn few, and more's the pity." - Red Pine Fishing Crew

"May the best of your past be the worst of your future!"

"Here's to the nights we'll never remember, with the friends we'll never forget."

"May the roof above these friends never fall in, and may the friends beneath this roof never fall out."

"May we never regret this."

Cheers!

Katharine Paulaha Brown

Notes & Recipes

Notes & Recipes

Notes & Recipes

Notes & Recipes

Notes & Recipes

The Author

Katharine Paulaha Brown received a B.A. in Journalism with minors in Business and Philosophy from the University of St. Thomas in Saint Paul, Minnesota, and, along with her skills in marketing, advertising, interior design, sales, negotiations, telecommunications, and real estate, has extensive hands-on knowledge and expertise in working with government licensing and regulatory agencies.

She currently works as a Sales Manager in the telecommunications industry, an industry in which she has an extensive background as well as both direct and indirect sales experience.

She is also a Realtor with a Graduate Real Estate Institute Certification (GRI) and is a member of the Minneapolis Area Association of Realtors (MAAR), the St Paul Area Association of Realtors (SPAAR), and the National Association of Realtors (NAR).

In the past, she worked for the largest daily deal-a-day company in the world, working with local restaurants, nurseries, dental offices, health and wellness companies, massage therapists, boat cruise lines, some of the oldest restaurants in Minnesota, and large international airlines.

In her free time, she enjoys skiing, party planning, interior design, remodeling projects, spending time on a beach, boating, camping, working in her garden, traveling, and cooking.

www.ingramcontent.com/pod-product-compliance
Lightning Source LLC
Chambersburg PA
CBHW050617110426
42813CB00008B/2592